Two Anxious Folk

Two Anxious Folk

✦

A Light-Hearted Look At A Serious Condition

Dr. Jekyll
and
Mrs. Hyde

iUniverse, Inc.
New York Lincoln Shanghai

Two Anxious Folk
A Light-Hearted Look At A Serious Condition

iUniverse books may be ordered through booksellers or by contacting:

iUniverse
2021 Pine Lake Road, Suite 100
Lincoln, NE 68512
www.iuniverse.com
1-800-Authors (1-800-288-4677)

www.jekyllandhydebooks.com

ISBN-13: 978-0-595-36569-2 (pbk)
ISBN-13: 978-0-595-80999-8 (ebk)
ISBN-10: 0-595-36569-8 (pbk)
ISBN-10: 0-595-80999-5 (ebk)

Printed in the United States of America

Contents

Foreword

This book is not intended to provide medical advice or serve as a substitute for medical treatment. It is intended as a book, a humorous, honest, and short book. Neither one of us is an expert in anxiety/panic disorder. However, both of us would entertain reasonable offers of playing one on T.V. In fact, we would most likely consider offers of playing anything on T.V.

As you may have surmised, we have chosen to use pseudonyms. It was a difficult decision that was met with resistance at all levels. In the end, we simply ignored everyone's perfectly logical arguments and went with what our gut told us. Still you may ask, "Why?" Fair enough.

Our reasons for anonymity:

•It adds to the mystique of the book.

We wholeheartedly support mystique in writing and the generous use of the word mystique in everyday conversation. Even our big hats and dark glasses on the back cover seem to add mystique. Mystique is derived from the classic Bulgarian word "*michticium*" which we understand to mean a rare furless rabbit that is indigenous to that area. Indeed furless rabbits are mysterious-just like us and this book.

•We were anxious.

Surprised? Don't be. Panic attacks are hard to describe and even harder for others to understand. There is still a stigma associated with them and we were flat out nervous about using our real names. Stigmas stink and we were unwilling to accept the consequences it could have for our family, friends and any future political aspirations we may develop. Other than our names, this is our writing, our thoughts, and our experience. If this book, at some point were to become wildly successful, or even develop a small cult following, we may reveal our real faces and identities. Until that time we will continue writing in disguise.

•It worked well for the theatrical rock band KISS.

Aside from extremely tall shoes that resemble demons and surgically enhanced tongues, we pretty much are following the same principle. This principle has also been adhered to by mimes, professional wrestlers, and James Bond. Let them know just a little about you and they will most likely want to know more.

Even though we chose anonymity this is still our story and our thoughts. Nothing has been changed except the names to protect the innocent.

Mrs. Hyde is a banker and may provide expert opinions on amortization, debt restructuring and commercial real estate loans. Dr. Jekyll, although a doctor, treats foot and ankle disorders and can provide expert opinions on broken ankles, bunions, and the anxiety associated with chronic athlete's foot. We pretend to be nothing other than your fellow panic attackers who choose to see panic disorder from a different view. That view being the same view a flock of birds has when flying over your freshly washed car.

This book should not be construed as "making fun" of the disorder. Ok, it is making fun of it. We have been down the same road, or at least a similar road, that all of you have and realize that it is frightening and potentially debilitating. It is our hope and prayer that this small contribution to the vast world of literature, while it may not reveal mind-numbing statistics and magical techniques, will make you smile. Hopefully, at some point, you will be able to look back and actually laugh. As an added bonus, we promise that you will never see the terms "alpha state" or "transcendental meditation".

Some may argue that we do not handle the topic with respect. We agree. It is our goal to offer it no respect and to tackle it with intense sarcasm, mockery, and the highest level of intolerance we can muster. If you are looking for another dark and somber book about this subject then we invite you to place this book near your freshly washed car.

Introduction

Your two fellow sufferers of panic disorder write this book. Although we found numerous academic texts helpful in educating us about the condition, our most informative books came from people who actually walked the walk. They seemed to brighten the light at the end of the tunnel. Thus, since we have also walked the walk we would now like to talk the talk.

Our purpose is not to cure you. We can't do that. Legally, ethically, and realistically we encourage you to seek medical help. This book seeks solely to be an aid in your journey towards overcoming panic disorder. And that, our dear jittery friends, is the good news—it is a journey, but most journeys do eventually end. The road may be rough and riddled with sharp stones that will leave your feet bleeding, but in the majority of cases the bleeding stops and you are finally able to rest your bare feet on the comforting grass of psychological peace.

We thought that books on anxiety were lacking. Not lacking in the sense of describing the disorder or the appropriate treatment, but lacking in a sort of quasi-encouraging, humorous sort of way. Some may argue that no physical or mental impairment should be mocked. We disagree. In this book we mock heavily. Panic disorder deserves to be mocked because it is a foul, nasty condition that can ruin lives. Keep in mind dear reader that we have been exactly where you are and we have recovered. That gives us the right to make fun of the condition because in a way we are laughing at ourselves. Although we are not academically experts, it is a fact that we stepped in the cow pie of anxiety and came out with clean shoes. That makes us experts—of sorts.

Our book is not intended to be a cure-all book. There are several self—help books produced by notable clinicians. We urge you to look to these for guidance. Besides these texts, it seems many people have developed novel websites arguing that they have stumbled upon some new fail proof way of dealing with this disorder. The colors of the website may be pretty. The graphics may be enchanting. In the end, most of them would encourage you to purchase something. This is not our goal. Granted, if this book makes us incredibly wealthy we will accept the royalty checks without hesitation. But, our main purpose in this short book is to let you know that we have been exactly where you are and to make you laugh. If we successfully cause you to soil yourself and forget about panic attacks for a few minutes we will have achieved our goal.

This book begins by introducing panic attacks. That is the first thing that you will be convinced you don't have. You'll call yourself a nut, section 8, crazy, loony and you are at least for now. You will be convinced you are going insane. Terms such as bipolar, psychotic, and schizophrenic will race through your mind and no one that has not been educated on the subject or has suffered with it can even start to understand. Don't worry. Read on and your anxiety will lessen just from removing the fear of the unknown. If by chance you do not receive comfort, ask the asylum attendant for a solid white straight jacket (as the gray straight jackets foster a more melancholy mood) and avoid sitting next to any patient that acts like a monkey and throws mashed potatoes.

Later on in the book we will discuss stress. Stress is a large component in this disorder and is often found to be the triggering factor. Gather as many books as you can on this condition and all of them will deal endlessly with this topic. Our goal will not be to bludgeon you with this subject, but to share our insight into stressors and how these can initiate or worsen anxiety. In simple terms the less stressed you are the less anxious you are. As your two authors and respective spouses often gather for relaxing herbal teas, croissants, and foot massages they are known to often quote the ancient proverb: "A person can only be as stressed as they allow themselves to be". Keep in mind though that your authors get together for very small reasons such as sampling strange and exotic fondue recipes and watching *American Idol*.

Towards the end we will discuss all of the strange and bizarre mind games that your body will treat you to. Your nose will grow. People will see you differently. Your eyes will no longer line up evenly. Your heart will explode numerous times. Your tongue will stick to your teeth. You will have medicine head feelings and you may think you have body odor. In addition you may have disturbing thoughts. All of these will initially convince you of your impending psychosis. Keep reading. You're still normal, but you may really stink.

The sensitive topic of medication will be approached. It will be obvious that we avoid specific mention of drug names, but rather focus on the benefits of medication. If you have scanned websites that deal with this disorder you have undoubtedly come across numerous links promising relief without medication. We cannot speak for those sites or for those who have benefited from them. We can speak for ourselves and assure you that medication in our case helped a great deal. Almost all sufferers of panic disorders try desperately to avoid prescriptions. This is normal. We all want to feel empowered and able to manage without pharmaceutical aid, but guess what? Most people can be helped tremendously with temporary use of medication. Although different clinicians may or may not prescribe medication, we want to introduce how medicine may be used as an adjunctive treatment. This will hopefully provide you with more insight into the medications you may be prescribed than the insight Forest Gump had when considering his box of chocolates.

In order to provide interesting variety to what could otherwise become a dry topic, we have asked our spouses to contribute to the "bystander" chapter of this book. Although we asked both spouses to help only Mrs. Hyde's husband took us up on the offer. Dr. Jekyll's wife just threw mashed potatoes at us so we just left her alone. This chapter not only provides an important perspective on the condition, but it also serves to educate our readers and encourage understanding about what our spouses, friends, and nosey neighbors—who have no life of their own—may be feeling. We have added a few bytes of wit and wisdom into this section to remind us that this disorder affects more than one person. Ideally, you will find ways to support your panic attacker, but if not, we can definitely provide numerous examples of how to stifle their recovery and completely push them over the edge.

Our two short stories conclude this book. Our particular onsets, symptoms, and most importantly recovery will be presented. Mrs. Hyde suffered from recurrent thoughts of impending death, whereas Dr. Jekyll was hounded by disturbing thoughts (Far worse than driving off without paying for your gas, switching price tags on desired garments, or secretly desiring to have benefited from the United Nations "oil for food scandal".). Each of these succeeded in causing multiple attacks, but in a different way. Remember our stories are not presented to convince our readers how perfect we are, but so that someone reading may stop and say, "Hey. I do that. I'm going to be ok, just like these two."

The most important thing to remember, whether you are the bystander or the one affected, is that everyone will have different symptoms. If you were to gather 100 anxious people you would most likely find 100 different physical, mental, and psychological manifestations of the disorder. (This should not be confused with stacking 100 anxious people on top of one another—which we would call "high anxiety".) What we have provided is just a few of the symptoms that we have had. Even though they vary, there is usually a common theme.

Above all we try to encourage each and every reader to keep a positive outlook. Granted we have both had multiple days in which happiness was not even pronounceable, much less obtainable. In reality this may be the main purpose of this text. It may not yield mountainous portions of information, but at the very least it may cause you to look up from beneath the belly of the anxiety goblin and simply smile. As the panic goblin tears ceaselessly at your emotions causing your mind to seem to shred, if you can for one second glance past the sharp claws of irrationality and focus on the peaceful blue background behind the horrid beast we will have been successful. Oh...and if you soil yourself.

The Anxiety Goblins

Many people may actually have a panic attack in their lifetime, but it actually takes more than one of these attacks (or a constant fear of having these attacks) in order to be diagnosed with panic disorder. To begin with, let us suggest that you not feel alone. Besides you and the two authors of this book, anxiety disorder affects approximately 15% of the U.S. population. If tens of millions of Americans actually have a true disorder and others have suffered at least one panic attack at some point, then you are in with a large group of people that can understand. This does not even include the rest of the civilized and uncivilized world. Often it will affect what is called a "Type A" personality. Everyone should take comfort in this last statement. When panic initially attacks we all feel tarnished and somehow begin to label ourselves as "weak". In actuality, this condition most often affects very driven, goal-oriented individuals. So pat yourself on the back. You're not weak…you're strong. You're too strong. So strong you've caused yourself problems.

Let us all step back for a few moments and look at who we are. Do you constantly need to be in control? Do you tend to initiate activities instead of following along? Do you always feel you need to be active in something or are you able to actually sit and "do nothing"? Do you have a few panic attacks and convince yourself that you need to write an entire book on the subject? Don't feel bad…we're the same way. When both of your authors and their respective spouses travel in the same minivan typically 5 minutes pre-travel time is allotted for wrestling for the driver's seat. (It's similar to the professional wrestling you undoubtedly watch on television only with more clothing, less emphasis on belittling your opponent, and no screaming announcements about whom you are taking on in the next match.)

When you are officially diagnosed, or suspect you will be, your greatest asset is knowledge. It has been said that nothing is feared as much as the unknown and that is most certainly true in our experience with panic disorder. Arming yourself with information serves three great purposes in our opinion. One—It reinforces that you are still most certainly mentally competent to function in society. (This includes endorsing checks, interacting socially, and operating heavy machinery.)

Two—It reminds us that we are not alone. Many people suffer to varying degrees. That's one of the reason we wrote this book. We have spouses. We have children. We have jobs. We are just like you. We're not alone and you're not alone. Three—the more you understand about the problem the easier it is to deal rationally with it, to confront it, and to master it. You begin to realize that what once seemed overwhelming is now still a difficult, but manageable, foe. This foe we liken to the old middle-age fairy tales about goblins. (Is there anything that is more anxiety causing than a goblin? Ok, bounced check fees and the unreasonable emphasis on low carbohydrate diets.)

When your authors began constructing this prime piece of literary art they discovered that multiple opinions existed as to causes and treatments for this condition. One thing that we did find was a common group of anxiety disorders that people who suffer from panic attacks can have as well. These are all closely related and we will deal only briefly with each of them. Again, we remind the readers that this is not intended to be an exhaustive work concerning this condition. Consider it rather…an introduction.

Anxiety is not bad. Anxiety that is chronic and alters your life is bad. The American Psychiatric Association has defined in the *Diagnostic and Statistical Manual of Mental Disorders* eleven anxiety disorders. They are as follows:

General Anxiety Disorder: chronic anxiety that continues for at least six months. This particular person does not have the typical phobias, obsessions, and does not experience panic attacks.

Obsessive-Compulsive Disorder (O.C.D.): this one really strikes home with your authors. We lived our lives assuming that everyone else in the world counted words in conversations, observed a ritualistic approach to coffee making, and those who did not enjoy these character traits were approaching life in a lazy, hap-hazard way. O.C.D. is usually thought of as "having" to perform some task such as washing your hands repeatedly. Although it does include this type of behavior, it also includes recurrent thoughts that can be unsettling and outright disturbing. We recall reading about a person obsessed with the fear of lobsters even though she lived nowhere near salt water. The fear was absolutely paralyzing for her. It is difficult for most of us to understand this irrational fear, but many panic attackers suffer from similar versions of this.

Post-traumatic Stress Disorder: has received much publicity over the past century as media coverage of global conflicts has increased. It involves psychological problems following a traumatic event.

Acute stress disorder is a response to a traumatic event, but usually resolves within weeks. Dr. Jekyll has this monthly when he writes his student loan repayment check.

Specific phobias are exactly what they sound like, a strong fear of a particular thing, act, or place. This is probably the most well known of the phobias. Many people cannot stand to fly. Some people fear bridges. Both of your authors are thankful that the only phobias we suffer from are perfectly acceptable. These include phobias about rising taxes, bed mites, and the increasing number of television reality series.

Social phobia can be specific or generalized. A generalized social phobia would cause the person affected to avoid any type of social setting. Naturally this would make selling cosmetics, vacuum cleaners, and cookies door to door virtually impossible. A specific version of this might include public speaking. In our research the fear of using public toilets is also listed as an example in several of our sources. We disagree completely. Any fear of placing your unclothed body where complete strangers have been unclothed is, in our opinion, perfectly normal. We choose to use only our own restrooms.

Agoraphobia, not to be confused with angoraphobia (the fear of lop-eared rabbits—which we surmise would be a specific phobia) can mean the fear of open spaces. Used more appropriately it means the fear of having a panic attack. Some people have referred to this as "the fear of the fear". From our perspective this is a horrible feeling. Imagine being fearful of being fearful. It's a circular problem. Because of this feeling, it is not uncommon for people with panic disorder to avoid certain "triggers" that seem to cause this feeling. These can become problematic quickly if they involve important functions such as driving, working, sleeping, eating, or breathing. In your research you will see that is why many people can become agoraphobic in the sense of shutting themselves off from the outside world.

General medical conditions can also induce anxiety disorders. These usually involve thyroid abnormalities, although heart problems and neurologic conditions have also been reported.

Substance—induced anxiety disorders can result from use or misuse of prescription medications. It can also be a result of medication interaction or withdrawal from one or more prescriptions. Recreational drugs can also induce severe forms of anxiety disorders.

There is also a small portion of the population that lives with agoraphobia with no history of concurrent panic attacks.

The final category, which is our primary focus, is panic disorder. Remember it takes more than one attack during a defined period or a constant fear of having another attack to actually constitute having a "disorder". Numerous authors can provide lists of what is typically experienced during an acute panic attack. In our individual stories later in the book you will receive an actual blow-by-blow of what happens during the attack…at least our attacks. Heart palpitations, sweating hands, a feeling of suffocation, out of body sensations, despair, and intense terror can all be involved. You will also see, or experience, the overlap of some of the phobias. Naturally, just like we did, you want to know why your body reacts this way.

The nervous system is composed of a voluntary and an involuntary segment. Aptly labeled, the voluntary system contracts muscles for walking, allows you to move your mouth to speak, and do that Russian dance in which the arms are folded across the chest and you kick one leg out straight at a time. The involuntary system maintains breathing, dilates or constricts your pupils, and clenches your gluteus maximus when you jump into frigid water. This last system can be further divided into sympathetic and parasympathetic. Parasympathetic regulates or promotes homeostasis or a better word might be "normalness". Sympathetic involves the controls that function when we are anxious or excited. It is this portion that is essentially out of control in panic disorder.

The amygdale is an interesting center within the human brain. One of its main functions is assisting other structures within your brain to essentially cause panic. Specifically, it plays a role in our "flight or fight response". When threatened we either defend ourselves or run away. (Some of us may run away while simply threatening to defend ourselves. Especially if a giant lobster is involved.) This response functions exactly as its name implies. When the amygdale is stimulated it causes your body to ready itself for an intense situation. For example, a racing heart and sweaty palms would be a normal reaction when the Velcro on your athletic shoes loosens during the "running of the bulls" in Pamplona, Spain. (We would even propose that an acute panic episode would be acceptable in this situation.) It is not, however, a normal reaction when you simply walk out the front door of the home you have lived in for years. The difficulty for people who have not experienced a panic attack is to understand how someone can perceive danger or dread when it is simply not there. Trust us, its frustrating for both parties involved.

Given the "hit and run" method of panic attacks, we choose to describe its method of recurrence as that of a goblin. The anxiety goblin is like any other of the goblins from old fairy tales. It doesn't confront you in the light. It doesn't run head long towards you and frontally assault you. What it does is it waits. It hides. It peeks from behind trees and waits to snatch you when you least expect it. We know it's unnerving. That is what makes panic disorder so troublesome. (Remember "the fear of the fear".) This is the constant tension of not knowing when it will happen. But let us give you a different perspective. We can't make the anxiety goblin go away, right now, but we can assure you that it does not have teeth. It does not have claws. Although it may attack you, ultimately it cannot physically harm you. That is what is so difficult for people to understand. In many cases you have the sense of physical harm approaching, but if for a few minutes you can step back, breathe deeply and remember…I'm still alive, you have won a large part of the battle. Even though the attack may have been horrendous it does eventually pass. It is simply a goblin without teeth. It can most certainly scare you. It can unnerve you. It can make you not want to leave your home. It can make you fearful, but it cannot physically "gobble you up". Our quote for you—and remember we've been there—"…it may scare you, but it won't kill you."

In your reading, you have probably uncovered the reassurance of authors who state repeatedly "…it may scare you, but it won't kill you." What we are trying to articulate is simply that once you have experienced panic attacks and then educated yourself about them, they become less and less powerful. In fact we found that "setbacks" (you know, taking two steps forward and one back) is more frustrating than it is scary. Feeling the symptoms that are a natural part of the human body's reaction to "impending danger" (Even though we all know that the danger is really not there.) such as a racing heart, sweaty palms, slurred speech, etc. can become less intimidating when you stop thinking, "I must stop this." You begin learning to relax, breath, and let these symptoms simply pass. They may pass in a few minutes. They may pass in a few hours, but eventually they will pass. We found the more we fought the symptoms—the more the symptoms multiplied—exponentially. Similar to rabbits in separate cages—somehow there are more of them two weeks later and your not quite sure how.

It's hard to stop trying to control the anxiety goblin. You want to hog tie him, drag him to a closet and lock him in there so he can't get out again. Then you look at him through the keyhole to make sure he's still in there. It may even be tempting to straighten a clothes hanger and try poking him through the keyhole just out of spite. Oh, he may be in there, but he's plotting to get out. Sometimes, you have to use psychological warfare on the beast. When the anxiety or panic is beginning to swell, you have to focus on what your fear is at that moment. Ask yourself the following questions:

What is the worst thing that can happen if this fear comes true?

What is the likelihood that this fear will come true?

Am I being realistic in my fear?

How can I face this logically?

Go to your happy place. We all have a thought that makes us happy, the one that makes all bad things go away. Seize that thought and focus on it. Everyone has a different happy place, for some it's the beach, others-big fluffy clouds. Mrs. Hyde sings "I Can See Clearly Now the Rain is Gone," in her head, over and over. Dr. Jekyll's vehicle to a happy place is the Jesus Prayer, "Lord Jesus Christ, Son of God, have mercy on me."

The one thing you have to remember is that all fairy tales have happy endings. The anxiety goblin in your fairy tale will eventually go away. He may go kicking and screaming, but he'll go. (Just for fun, we suggest that you poke him one more time with the hanger as he is leaving.) And you all will live happily ever after.

Good, Bad, and Ugly Stress

Everyone always assumes that stress is bad. Losing a job, illness, gaining weight, slowly watching your hairline recede, and increasing reliance on medication to enhance intimacy are all examples of what today's society does to push us closer to the snarling goblin of anxiety. In reality stress can also be good. What we mean is that stress is easily defined as any type of change. What is most important is how we handle stress. Some researchers distinguish between eustress and distress. In our non-expert opinion, we understand eustress to basically mean that stressful situations are handled well. Distress means the situation is not handled well. Let us explain with the same story, but two drastically different outcomes.

Melvin, your regular attendant at Hoffbraugh Latte Hut has recently quit. For the past 8 months Melvin has greeted you with a smile, a pleasant introduction and a healthy froth on top of your caffeine laden beverage. It's routine. It's stability. It's the start of another bird-chirping, sun shining morning. But one day Melvin is gone. Why? Who knows? Never the less he's gone.

Horace assumes Melvin's position. At first you are skeptical. Why? The first reason is because most of us are creatures of habit and two, because you find anyone with the name of Horace suspicious. Change is unsettling. You soon find that Horace also greets you with a pleasant smile, a handshake, and an even more ample layer of froth. You quickly forget Melvin and embrace your new latte artist Horace. But it's still change. It's still stress. It's not the routine. In no way is it bad, but it still is stressful because it is new. Not bad, just new.

But what if Melvin resigns and now Billy (the "Billster" as he encourages you to call him) fills your latte half full, skimps on the froth, and insists on rubbing your shoulders while you find the correct change in your purse. To top it all off, as he is Rolfing you at 6:42 a.m. he whispers "Man I wish I had the secret pin number to your ATM card." This too is stressful in a flagrant almost assaulting sort of way.

As you can see, both of these scenarios cause stress. One is actually good and the other is obviously bad, but both of them force emotional changes within our minds. How we respond to the situation categorizes it is as either eustress or distress. It is the constant build up of these "stressors" that eventually trigger a classic panic attack. Weddings, funerals, job losses, job gains, are diametrically opposite to one another, but still can contribute equal, but different types of stress. Thinking back on all of our "first attacks", most are described as "coming out of the blue", but in hindsight, many of us are able to identify a building of stress (good or bad) that contributed. Cumulative stress has been described as a build up of unreleased stress over a period of months or years. Stress that has been effectively dealt with is not allowed to accumulate.

Experts point out that "bad" stress can be lumped into three different categories. ACUTE stress is simply what its name implies. It has a quick onset and dissipates just as rapidly. This type of stress may include misplacing your car keys, burning cheese fondue, and finally realizing that the "hygienic" toilet seat covers in public restrooms provide little if any protection. In all of these examples, the problem arises but is quickly gone. You may suffer a headache, backache, stomach upset, and become irritable, but there are no lasting effects.

The next category is defined as ACUTE EPISODIC stress. All of us know someone who is chronically late or is a constant worrier. This type of person always misplaces car keys, always burns cheese fondue, and has developed possible theories about conspiracies involving misrepresentation of disposable toilet seat covers. (In the next book your authors may propose certain of these theories, which involve complicated financial relationships between the Merovingians and indigenous Eskimo tribes of the Alaskan Islands.) This type of stress will actually cause more physical manifestations in the person. These manifestations move past headaches and become migraines. They may also begin to develop regular gastrointestinal problems.

The final category is defined as CHRONIC stress and it is the most serious of the three. This is unrelieved stress that will eventually cause physical or psychological illness. (Remember that it can accumulate.) The human body is created to handle certain levels of stress for certain periods of time. Problems arise when that threshold is exceeded. You authors liken it to the shell of an egg...squeeze it too much and the shell cracks...squeeze it even harder and your yoke runs out. (Trust us; you do not want your psychological yoke running all over the place.)

Stress can be the initial and recurrent trigger for panic attacks. In hindsight, most of us can see many stressful events that were building prior to the beginning of our panic episodes. Rarely is it one definable event, but rather a gathering of events that edges us over the anxiety cliff. Throughout your panic attack journey, you will also find that stressful situations can initiate an attack. This can often be legitimate stress such as car wrecks and financial strain, but it can also begin to be—what we call "*Illegitimate stress*"—things that typically would not be stressful or would be only faint possibilities of being stressful. Examples might include stressing about having a wreck when you have not actually had a wreck or feeling you may physically harm someone when you have absolutely no history of harming anyone. This is what is so difficult for people who have not had a true panic attack to understand. The thought of something quickly turns into a perceived reality. In the end, we have found that reducing stress can help decrease the number and severity of panic attacks.

After much thought—and slight laughter—your authors make simple suggestions for reducing stress. Prior to implementing any of our suggestions we suggest you seek clearance from family, friends, religious leaders, physicians, lawyers, financial advisors, and your local weather person. Some of the techniques below are ones that have been successfully employed by both of us, some we have read about in our research, and some are for entertainment purposes only (but sound like they would be pretty effective).

"Have to do." "Need to do." "Like to do." These need to be defined and then redefined. We found that a short bout with panic attacks can often provide an incredible amount of clarity when it comes to evaluating and setting priorities. For example, mental peace and maintaining family ties is far more important than wealth acquired after working 120 hours a week. Prioritizing and eliminating unnecessary activities can help reduce the amount of chronic stress that each of us endures. It is unfortunate that it takes a disorder such as this to cause us to take a step back and evaluate what is most important in life.

Visit petting zoos. Spending time with non-violent animals such as fish, swans and goats is calming as well as educational. In our research, spending time with violent animals such as lions, dingoes and asps may actually exacerbate chronic anxiety. For proof of this theory, you may want to examine medication lists for various zoo workers.

Exercise can be good and exercise can be bad. In short, "all things in moderation". Regular exercise can reduce the risk of chronic disease, increase a positive self image, and reduce stress and/or help us deal more effectively with it. However, because it also can affect the body's hormones, it can also worsen the tendency for recurrent attacks if approached fanatically. The readers are invited to research the topic of "exercise induced panic attacks".

Educate your self on the affliction. Although historically people have argued that ignorance is the best medicine, this could not be further from the truth when it comes to panic disorder. Knowledge is your weapon of defense in the recovery process. Knowing how many people also suffer with this, how many people have recovered, and the symptoms that accompany it is half of the battle.

Diet is an often neglected, but in our humble opinion important, aspect of managing this disorder. Foods, and certain chemicals contained therein, can affect the function of your body. Caffeine is often touted as a great evil in many different conditions. We find it unrealistic to try and convince you that caffeine should be completely eliminated from your daily regimen. If you consider that it is a stimulant then understandably any reduction in the amount of stimulation you receive should lessen the factors contributing to an attack. One of your authors, Dr. Jekyll, has found there is a very direct correlation between certain amounts of caffeine and physiologic response within his body. To illustrate, he completely and quickly gave up caffeine during his first week of panic attacks. This was a bold move given the fact that he typically consumed 2–3 cups of coffee each morning and 88 ounces of diet cola throughout the day. This abrupt cessation in caffeine consumption was not intentional, but in reality because he felt he was becoming psychotic and coffee and cola drinking simply fell quickly to the bottom of his priority list. This now seems ridiculous—knowing what he now knows—and also because truly psychotic people still seem to enjoy coffee, colas, and occasional mochachinos. His mild setbacks, even after beginning treatment, coincided directly with excessive caffeine consumption. "Half—caff" and he was fine. Regular coffee or energy drink and heart palpitations started. In all likelihood the palpitations were unrelated to anxiety, but since he had experienced these as initial stages in a panic attack he would quickly move towards a full blown attack. Eventually he learned to focus on keeping caffeine to a respectable level and when symptoms began he finally became comfortable saying, "Whatever." Prior to arriving at the point where he was incredibly nonchalant with these symptoms, he remains most certainly sure that to an outsider he must have been clutching his chest and staggering about like Fred Sanford and announcing that he would soon be meeting Elizabeth. Also, your authors can attest, many of the classes of medicine that you may be prescribed can cause drowsiness so giving up all caffeine may be easier said than done. Cut back. Watch at what times you use it. Switch to half-caff.

The word relaxation could not possibly be used more when reading about panic attacks. Numerous books, articles, and websites seem to promote everything from magic beans to flatulence enhancing techniques. (Granted we have not personally tried flatulence enhancing techniques, but assume that the "enhanced" portion of the technique may directly correlate with the magic beans.) Every individual will actually need to experiment with certain methods to see which actually work best in their particular case. One of the simplest tasks to master is actually setting aside a certain period in each day (or multiple periods) to simply do nothing, but close your eyes and breathe deeply. This doesn't have to be a meditative session, but focusing on positive thoughts can often enhance deep breathing and relaxation of tense muscles.

Consider prayer for a moment. Many of us who have suffered from anxiety disorders received a great deal of relief through a conscious and consistent prayer life. Granted it may not have been perfect, but it was most definitely an essential part of our recovery. Some may argue that what actually benefits those praying is simply relaxation, rhythmic breathing, and focusing during that time period. We would counter that this may indeed be partially the case, but it is our firm belief that prayer also serves the more important purpose of communing with the Creator of the human race, who, we are certain, is not anxious.

Irrational Thinking

You're brain is your friend. When a good friend deserts you, disappoints you, or runs away from you screaming—it can be disheartening. Think of your brain as a well—oiled machine, much like your car. (Some people drive luxury cars others ride mopeds.) We're not quite sure how it works, much like your car, but if you get your oil changed frequently, get a tune up, obey recall notices when they are issued (i.e.: panic attacks) it usually can carry you where you want to go for years. So what causes a recall notice? A variety of things can, but if you refer back to our chapter on stress you can usually pinpoint for yourself where it all went tragically wrong.

The problem builds for a good period of time and potentially you ignore it. Who are we kidding, not potentially, you do. Your stress builds to inhuman levels and you are not sure what to worry about first or most. You become concerned about weird little things. This phase is fondly known as "Analysis Paralysis". You don't know what to think or do, so you just continually roll it over in your mind and take no action whatsoever.

Have you ever had a conversation with someone and when it's over, you both laugh and say, "Now, how did we get from there to here?" If you replay one of your panic attacks in your head, you will ask the same question. We'll give you an example.

The room is so crowded and so loud. One of your husband's co-workers catches your eye and starts to walk over. Inside your head you're screaming, "Run, run while you have the chance. I can't feel my hands. I can't feel my hands! Come to think of it, I can't feel my nose either. I wonder if they know that I can't feel my nose or my hands. What will happen if they know? Will my husband be upset with me because they know I'm a freak? Smile, smile and make eye contact for the love of God. By the way, God, I so need you right now, please help me. What if God can't hear me, what if he doesn't care anyway? Breathe, breathe, am I visibly hyperventilating? I feel like I'm visibly hyperventilating. Wow, my heart is beating so fast. Could my heart possibly beat so fast that it will explode? Oh, how sad, what will happen to my husband and my son if my heart explodes in my chest right here? Oh, seriously, you're heart is not going to explode right here. Is that fear reasonable? No, get a hold of yourself."

The co-worker reaches out and shakes your hand, "Hi, I'm John; I work with your husband."

"Nice to meet you, I'm his wife," you say in your controlled voice, the neither a freak nor having a panic attack voice.

"He's a super guy, he talks about you all the time," John says.

"Oh, I'm sure he does," you banter back. Then you immediately think, "Now why would I say something like that, I've just let on to him that I'm weird and my husband has good reason to talk about me. This is excruciating." You smile politely; knowing that your lips are sticking to your teeth and now, your eye has started to twitch.

John gives you a meager grin and says, "It was very nice meeting you, I'm sure we'll run into each other later."

"You bet, it was nice to meet you too," you respond, now very focused on the fact that not only is your nose numb, but it feels like its growing. And all the while, wondering what John just thought of your whole interchange. You're pretty sure he thinks you're crazy. Which truly is your biggest fear, you just realize. You're afraid you're going crazy and with the panic that has just risen inside you over meeting poor John, you're pretty sure you're not going, but gone.

Does this feel familiar at all? That whole internal interchange is a classic example of how your irrational thinking can run away with you. You may have noticed what we have noticed. Although these goblins can blind-side you at any time, this seems to occur most often when you don't have something to occupy your mind. "An idle mind is the devil's workshop." (Now that is a statement that is prime fodder for irrational thinking.) Therapists often point out that one of the most common times for people to seek help with panic attacks is Sunday afternoon. This makes perfect sense when we consider that for many people this is usually a quiet non-demanding portion of the week.

So You Are A Serial Killer…Now What?

This section is really more of a continuation of the previous chapter. It is important to remember that all people with panic attacks will have different symptoms. Some may have visual disturbances, some a "medicine head" feeling and many others. One of the least talked about topics is that of disturbing thoughts. We are perplexed as to how to actually tackle this subject light-heartedly because it can be a very troubling experience. It seems to be the least discussed because no one wants to admit to themselves, much less to someone else, that they have had thoughts like these.

One of the things that may occupy your time is how does a person go from normal to, let's say, a serial killer? We've all watched the news reports on T.V., all the neighbors say, "He seemed very normal, but always kept to himself. We had no idea he had 10 bodies buried in his backyard and was that fond of chocolate." Since neither of us is a serial killer—although we would consider playing one on T.V.—we wonder how you can appear normal and be a serial killer? Good question. Unfortunately we don't have the answer. If only it were true that all serial killers had really widely spaced eyes and low set ears. But the research we've done, from watching dozens of documentaries on serial killers, leads us to the following conclusion. You may have odd thoughts; the fact that you are concerned over your odd thoughts is the blessing you need to cling to desperately. Serial killers aren't concerned, they definitely don't think they are crazy and they often think they are smarter than everyone else. To all those reading that have had a panic attack you must remember how you feel about yourself in those moments of doubt; you <u>are</u> concerned, you <u>truly believe</u> your crazy and your intelligence <u>is</u> <u>questioned</u> at every corner of your anxious brain. See, sometimes being anxious comes in handy.

Recurrent disturbing and irrational thoughts are the most annoying, frustrating, and potentially disabling symptoms that you can suffer from. From the start, take comfort in the fact that many experts estimate that approximately 75% of people who have recurring panic attacks have these uncontrolled thoughts.

Uncontrolled thoughts can range from absurd themes such as feeling your speech is slurred to more morbid thoughts such as worrying that you may have an uncontrollable urge to run over someone on the sidewalk. It is important for readers to understand that you do not actually have an urge to run over someone, but you have a fear that you will have an urge to run over someone. (To those of you who have not had a panic attack there simply is no good way to explain this.) The difficult thing about irrational thoughts is that they tend to feed off one another. As soon as we are successful in ousting one bag of garbage from our mental attic, three bags seem to take its place. It is unnerving, especially at the onset of panic attacks, to have these strange thoughts. It is most likely completely out of character for you. Don't worry you're not a sociopath.

Managing negative thoughts is a task that eventually becomes an automatic response. At first though, and we empathize with you, it can be one of the most difficult things you have ever attempted. To give you an analogy, consider hearing a song on the radio or television and then being unable to stop singing it over and over involuntarily. These thoughts are similar to the energizer bunny…the keep going and going and going….

The whole concept behind management of these thoughts is not to simply wrestle repeatedly with them, but to replace them with positive alternatives. For example, rather than worrying that you may one day collapse mentally and crave human flesh approach the thought calmly as illustrated previously. Ask yourself the following:

Have I ever craved human flesh?

How likely is it that I would crave human flesh now?

Has anyone in my family ever craved human flesh?

How can I handle my perceived craving for human flesh logically?

Wouldn't beefalo or emu meat be a more healthy alternative?

Naturally we would provide the most ridiculous thought we could find to amplify a point. The point is that these irrational thoughts are so outlandish they make no sense. In fact, to illustrate the absurdity even more, write down the thought and then write down the steps of rationalizing the thought. (Mrs. Hyde provides a wonderful example of her husband, Mr. Hyde, actually sitting down with her and listing her irrational thoughts and why they were irrational.) As you progress, you'll find that you will skip the actual process of reasoning through the irrational thought and skip directly to the "this is ridiculous" statement at the end. Some people may actually have a spouse that skips the rationalization process and proceeds immediately to the "this is ridiculous" stage. We won't say your ridiculous. Trying to tell someone who has panic attacks to "just forget about it" is like telling someone to stop sweating or a pregnant woman to stop craving or the government to stop taxing.

Dr. Jekyll was originally very disturbed when two days after his first panic attack he had a thought of suicide. Again you really don't have thoughts of performing the act itself. What you have is an irrational view of what happens if someday you snap and do it. You have a tremendous fear of <u>not</u> wanting to do it. This fear quickly turns into an obsession in which you try to rid this kind of thought from your mind. The more you attempt to shove this mental goblin, the more he bludgeons you. It's a vicious cycle…or a vicious circle.

Prior to panic attacks, Dr. Jekyll was an "eternal optimist". The mere thought simply popping into his head caused not only an increased level of anxiety, but also its close friend depression. It was dark cloud depression—the kind where there seems like there is no hope. We choose to call it the *Loch Ness Theory of Depression*. Even when you can't see it it's out there, somewhere, and eventually it will resurface. It seems odd now to think that a healthy 35 year old male, attractive, witty, smart, svelte and happily married for 14 years, three sons, and a successful medical practice could be depressed, but trust us it happened. Luckily the despair lasted only a day and returned only a few times prior to actually seeking treatment for the anxiety. Depression tends to be the bed-fellow to anxiety seemingly because you feel you are beginning to lose control and "nothing will ever be the same". Dr. Jekyll, don't stone him now, used to feel depression was mental weakness. A simple flip of the switch could make it all better. Having been mauled by it personally now, he apologizes profusely and empathizes with those who understand that it is a thick, fetid, fog that is difficult and often impossible to lift. Never feel you are unworthy, weak, or faulted in some way because you are depressed. It is just one more way your mind is crying for you to get help. Always tell someone when you feel depressed because it can be a sinking hole that just gets deeper the more you try to handle it alone. It's like quick sand. Let somebody know so they can toss you a rope.

Back to kitchen knifes and being scared of dress belts. Fear is really at the root of the anxiety and these irrational, disturbing thoughts. Anything that mentions someone being normal and then discovering that he or she kept women in pits can often cause the <u>fear</u> of doing the same thing. Notice we did not say the <u>desire</u> to do the same thing. In fact, you have such a loathing and disgust for this that you actually work yourself into a lather trying to avoid even the remote possibility that you would think in such a way. In a manner of speaking, people who suffer from anxiety disorder are really "too sane". As mentioned earlier, people who keep people in pits often fail to realize that it is socially inappropriate, whereas others of us most definitely realize that it is not the social norm.

Scared of accidentally hanging yourself with a dress belt? Normal. (A friend of mine who we just mentioned this to aptly said, "But that's not really normal." Point taken. Please understand that we use the term "normal" loosely to mean normal when dealing with panic disorder.) Have you been scared of attacking your left hand with a knife while cutting vegetables for Lentil soup? Been there. Scared of not loving your wife or kids when you know they mean the world to you? Done that also. It is all part of the thoughts and fears generated by the anxiety. Pick up any text or peruse most internet sites for anxiety and these will be common themes. As you increase your mental defenses to shield against these thoughts you become more and more anxious until you become comatose with alcohol or a readily available sedative.

Code Blue

This book does not discuss depression in detail but we would like to offer a short word on being blue.

Depression and panic disorder are, again, bedfellows. In our opinion, it is essentially impossible to have one without the other. This may be a result of the close link between neurotransmitters that control our nerve impulses within the brain. They also are linked due to the sudden and lingering aspects of the disorder. Most sufferers would agree that a seemingly bleak outlook caused by an uncontrollable condition (at least at first) can be extremely disheartening. That is one of the reasons we encourage everyone to seek help early. The longer the cycle continues the more difficult it becomes to break.

Code blue is a term used in a medical setting to announce that someone is having a cardiac arrest and all essential personnel should proceed to that area immediately. When suffering from depression picture yourself announcing to anyone that will listen what is going on inside your mind and those people within earshot running to your aid. Get help. It's good.

Strange Sensations

The human body is interesting and a delicate mix of multiple chemicals and reactions. Just think of how much attention all of us must pay to simply merge onto a crowded highway, mix a recipe appropriately, or dance the mamba. You can only imagine the millions of chemical messages that are sent and received everyday within the human brain—and that includes just thoughts. That does not even include messages sent for movement, breathing, digestion, etc.

Some people with anxiety disorders experience strange physical sensations along with the mental panic. Ever had your hands go numb when you're talking with someone? Ever had you're heart start to beat so quickly while you're sitting still that you think, "If I could do this everyday for 20 minutes, I wouldn't need aerobic exercise?" Ever been walking and not felt your body and then been afraid that it would forget to do what it was supposed to do and you would fall down? Ever been abducted by aliens for scientific experimentation, but they returned you due to the anxiety you caused the crew of the mother ship? Us either, we were just curious.

Nerve impulses travel across small gaps between different nerve segments called synapses. These impulses are transmitted via chemicals termed neurotransmitters. You may have stumbled across terms such as serotonin and dopamine. If neurotransmitters become depleted, from a host of reasons, you can experience numerous psychological manifestations such as irritability, confusion, inability to concentrate, and disturbing thoughts. Think of it as a net through which certain objects are sifted. When your net functions normally you are able to filter certain thoughts that are unacceptable. However, when the anxiety goblin molests your net, jagged holes may allow objects to drain through faster than you can collect them. The faster your little feet carry you to catch these foreign objects the faster they pour through. Finally, in mental exhaustion you realize that you and Ted Bundy have far too much in common. You admit in defeat that you have numerous attributes that are similar to his. You lie on the floor and visualize the check off list. "We both have two eyes! We both have hair! We both faired poorly in English class and wet the bed into our early teens!"

In response to this type of stimulation adrenaline is released. The majority of you are at least familiar with adrenaline. It is what stimulates you to fight or flee. You may have heard of someone lifting a car to free a loved one trapped beneath it. Adrenaline. You may have heard of someone bolting through a wall of fire to save a child. Adrenaline. You may have heard of someone being severely injured and not feeling pain. Adrenaline. You may have heard of the police shooting someone twelve times and that person falling out of a 6 story building, bouncing off of a metal dumpster and then running away laughing. That was not adrenaline. That was P.C.P. Adrenaline is responsible for the intensity felt when a panic attack is quickly approaching. Think of it as an electrical surge. We, as panic attackers, just happen to be standing barefoot in water holding a hair dryer.

Adrenaline affects numerous organs and systems within you body. It constricts blood vessels, it causes your heart to race; it causes you to have an intense feeling of a threat. It can make you sweat. It can alter your perception. It can give you a tingling sensation all over. To sum it up, adrenaline can essentially take any of your body's responses and morph it into something abnormal. It is difficult, actually it's impossible, to resist these symptoms. To mentally confront them and try to stop a physiologic response is a futile effort. Panic attackers are far more successful in acknowledging that these symptoms are a natural bodily response and waiting for them to pass. Relaxing, breathing, and accepting are more effective than trying to wrestle adrenaline. Eventually, through professional therapy, self-help therapy, and possibly medication these symptoms begin to fade away.

Bear in mind that at times all of us experience setbacks. A setback is a recurrence of these symptoms after we were convinced that they were mastered. Setbacks are like fish and visiting relatives…they both stink after a few days. As you recover from recurrent attacks, remember that your perception or "outlook" plays a pivotal role in the process. The way you view "bad days" needs to be changed. You cannot have a bad day unless you had a better day at some point prior to it. In other words, in the journey of panic disorder (Remember the one where your feet bleed?) setbacks simply come as a result of improvement. Mrs. Hyde can draw numerous analogies between "hopscotch recovery" and the bear and bull market fluctuations. Just think of what you do on a bad hair day—you throw a cap on and deal with it. Panic attacks are typically a culmination of weeks, months, or years of stressful events…expecting them to be resolved instantly is unrealistic and sets the stage for significant disappointment.

The Importance of Telling
Someone You May Be Psychotic

The conversation started casually enough. Dr. Jekyll walked into the house with a cup of tea in his hand, as he so often does after a run. Lots of thoughts flow after you've been working out and we're neighbors and good friends so anything is up for discussion.

"Have you ever known anyone who has panic or anxiety attacks?" He asked innocently, sipping his tea, pinky extended, chamomile wafting in the air.

"Well, me." Mrs. Hyde responded, feeling mildly uncomfortable, but not having anxiety because she is so over that now. "Why?"

"Well, the weirdest thing happened to me today." Dr. Jekyll began to tell a story that all of us have gone through. The first experience is always one of the most frightening. You're not really sure what just happened. You've seen this stuff on TV, "What nuts," you may have even thought to yourself. So when it happens to you, you're not quite sure how to react. Do I tell someone? Dare I ask if this has happened to anyone I know? This starts another bout of anxiety that you must fend off. Confession soothes the soul, finding someone you trust that doesn't think you are a nut is joy.

You do take a tremendous risk in telling someone this is happening to you. You expose yourself as weak, inadequate, irrational, unable to help yourself and potentially insane. That's what it feels like doesn't it? The reality is, it's the farthest thing from the truth. You reveal yourself as human. It's amazing how many people you know that this has touched. People who have been there will go out of their way to help you. It's a strange club, but a very tight knit one. No judgments are needed. Sympathy and patience are really what you need.

The best advice we received and the best we can give you is to go see a medical professional. The sooner you see one the better. They are specialists; they can evaluate you and plan a course of action that will relieve your worried mind. A lot of the anxiety comes from the fear that you will have another panic attack. Why torture yourself when there are very good medications that can relieve that bit of stress? It can also be very beneficial to have some time with a counselor, psychologist, psychiatrist, whomever you choose, to just talk through the situation and anything going on in your life. Someone who knows nothing about you and is totally objective can give you insights into yourself that you refuse to see. Did you know flicking the light switch seven times before leaving a room or making sure your coffee tastes the same every morning or it ruins your day could mean you're a little obsessive compulsive? Neither did we. See, the theory proves itself.

You do need to find someone to share your thoughts and fears with so you don't feel alone. This leads us to the term "safe people". These two words are commonly used in conjunction with panic disorder. This refers, obviously enough, to people that you cling to when you need support during an acute attack. It quickly expands to include these people at times in between attacks as well. During an actual attack, when the world is crashing down on you like a sumo wrestler's butt (sweat and pimples included), your safe person is someone that you feel you must have around. In an acute attack the last thing you want is to be left alone. When you begin to associate "triggers" with the onset of attacks you may become more and more dependant on these same people. "Tween people" we like to call them at that point. The desire to have these people around is driven by a need for support and comfort, but we have concluded that it also comes from a perception that the presence of this person may stave off another attack. In our humble opinion this seems to work because one: there is safety in numbers (Yes even two is more than one.) and two: they serve as a source of distraction. In a panic attack trying to rid yourself of a negative, intrusive thought is most difficult. When you have someone around you are naturally aided in this mental maneuvering.

The drawback to "safe" and "tween" (Maybe they should be called "real safe" and "somewhat safe".) is that it is very easy to cross the boundary separating support and dependence. At first it is comforting to have these people around, but quickly it can deteriorate into a necessity that they are around. Caring and supportive people can quickly become a crutch that is difficult to wean yourself from. In fact, the stress of your condition may cause your "crutch" to kick itself out from beneath you. In the end, all anxiety sufferers must realize that you have to stand on your own two feet and confront what you fear the most. If driving seems to trigger an attack—we must drive. If being in a social setting triggers an attack—we must place ourselves in that setting. Initially having "safe people" can provide comfort, but it should be our goal to gradually wean ourselves from them and be able to stand on our own. Remember…"all things in moderation"…even safe people.

Medication: Our Friend

When the Doctor tells you it's time for meds, you can have two possible reactions, we'll call them Mrs. Hyde's Response and Dr. Jekyll's Response. You may also choose to call them response A and response B. You may also call them nothing similar to your own response.

Mrs. Hyde's Response

It's totally official…I am crazy. So crazy in fact, that a totally rational Doctor, who sees people with problems every day, thinks I will benefit from "Anti-Anxiety" medication. What does that mean anyway? Do I act anxious? Is there something in my behavior that makes him think I'm anxious? All I did was tell him I can't be around people without my hands going numb and the fear that my heart is going to beat itself to both of our untimely deaths, that I can't keep weird thoughts from popping into my head or get them out once they are there. Pretty soon I'll be institutionalized, receive electroshock therapy and drool all over myself.

Dr. Jekyll's Response

Thank God! I am not going crazy. This happens to a lot of people. This medication is really going to work! (A short response, but effective.)

In case it isn't obvious, Dr. Jekyll's response is the appropriate one. For some people, it can be devastating to learn that you need medication to control your thoughts and how you react to stress. One of the moments when all you can see is the belly of the beast that is shredding your mind. For others, it's one moment of blue sky behind the ugly critter.

Just so you do not think that Dr. Jekyll had a picture perfect response to treatment, he freely admits that for two months he relied on prayer and scripture and it did help immensely, but the anxiety still lingered and it felt as though you had to always mentally guard your thoughts because at any moment you could drop off the precipice of anxiety and plunge head first into blatant insanity. When he finally chose to meet with a psychiatrist he honestly felt as though it was a statement on his lack of faith and failure as a Christian. What the medication actually did was allow him to return to sleeping, laughing, reading, and drawing closer to Christ.

Most of us would not consider avoiding medication when it comes to treating any other conditions. Think of it as a disease that can be treated successfully. Would we hesitate to take medication for pneumonia? Granted there are differences. Some would argue that people have been able to recover from pneumonia without medication, thus something that is not even truly an infection should be easily treatable without medication. We would in turn offer that although a small percentage of people may be capable of mounting a large enough immunologic response to recover without medication, the majority of people recover much more quickly with the aid of medication. The authors suggest that medication should not even be considered a treatment, but rather an aid or adjunct. It can often speed the recovery process.

Depending on the prescription, the effects can be immediate or can take weeks for the relief to become noticeable. What the medicine provides is respite from the unsettled mind, freedom from bouts of anxiety/panic and the ability to begin rewiring your thought process. Often, the ability to be rational is the biggest relief of all.

We know about the side affects, or should we say, what people will preach the side affects to be. So you're a little sleepy, so sex isn't your number one priority, so you can't operate heavy machinery—UNTIL YOU GET USED TO HOW THE MEDICATION AFFECTS YOU! These were all temporary. Giving up heavy machinery was very hard for us, and our spouses, but we were wielding chain saws and drills in short order and EVERYBODY was happy.

For us, the medication was not a permanent situation. Mrs. Hyde was on it for 9 months and Dr. Jekyll, having been dealing with panic disorder for only six months at the time of the manuscript writing, is still currently on the medication. As he improves, he trusts that he will also be able to crush his medication bottle against his forehead just like we all do with our empty beer cans.

It wasn't scary coming off the meds. (Dr. Jekyll doesn't really know, but we'll just suggest you take Mrs. Hyde's word for it.) By that time, you have learned to manage your thoughts. You have also, if you've taken this seriously, learned what makes you stressed and how to keep that to a minimum.

As we discussed before, managing negative thoughts is of utmost importance in dealing with panic disorder. You must learn that when a negative thought enters your mind it must immediately be removed and replaced with something positive. For example, we cannot tell how many times we experienced the thought, "You're not going to overcome this." We had to learn, and you will too, to instantly remind ourselves how much we had improved and that we would make it. We would overcome it. You will be very surprised that after enough repetition this will become an automatic response. Chances are it won't even hinder your use of heavy machinery.

Mrs. Hyde's Story

OK, here's the thing. I've pretty much known all my life I was a little "different". I counted the words in a conversation, on my fingers visually in my head, as I spoke with people. I had to end on my pinky or I got nervous. In Junior High, my morning routine had to be exactly the same or I fell apart. For a long time, I chalked it up to my childhood and a pretty strict father. The reality of it is I am a perfectionist. If I can't be perfect at it, I ain't gonna do it at all. This causes an extreme amount of stress because no one, with the exception of Jesus, is, was or will be perfect.

This perfectionism manifested itself into anxiety attacks when I had my son. Talk about being slapped in the face with the fact that you are miles away from perfect. Motherhood teaches you a lot about yourself. I discovered I was woefully inadequate. I was afraid I was failing, in a big way. His head was flatter on one side because I didn't rotate him enough, he spit up because I didn't breastfeed, he liked his Dad more than me, yada, yada, yada. It just continued to build until one day I called my Obstetrician and asked if I could come in. He asked me to fill out a questionnaire and one of the questions was "Do you have thoughts of suicide?". Seriously, a perfectionist that wants to kill herself, there's nothing perfect in that. I got a nagging thought that this guy thought I was crazy.

When I went into the exam room, he asked me several questions. I remember sharing that I had difficulty being around a lot of people, that my heart would race for no apparent reason, and I just had a general feeling of sadness and anxiousness. He recommended an anti-depressant that also helped with anxiety. I took the prescription and left. My life went to hell in a handbasket from there.

I had a 72 hour anxiety attack that weekend. I didn't eat for 3 days, which was fantastic for dropping pregnancy weight, but very, very wrong. I kept telling my husband to take me to the psych ward, that I was seriously going crazy. He kept telling me I wasn't and I really wanted to believe him. On Sunday, he sat me down on the kitchen floor with a piece of paper.

"Tell me the reasons why you think you are going crazy," he said. I immediately gave him 7 reasons. He looked at the list and started at the top. Item by item, he told me why that wasn't rational and crossed them off the list. The last item was that I couldn't eat. He looked me in the eyes and said, "If I have to sit on you and force you to eat, you will eat and you will realize you are not crazy." I bawled like a baby. One of my fears had been that he would leave me and in that moment, I knew that no matter how bad I got, he would always be with me, help me and love me. He told me he would set up an appointment with the counselor at his place of employment on Monday just to get an outside perspective. I agreed.

It was that weekend that I realized how much I missed having God in my life. I believe God has a plan for all of us and sometimes it takes extreme circumstances for us to come back to him. I hadn't been to church in years, but there was a gaping hole in me I needed to fill. I remember clinging to the thought that God could get me through it.

I went and saw the counselor on Monday, I was terribly uncomfortable. I felt like my anxiety was an enormous zit on my face. Not the kind of zit that hasn't erupted yet, but the kind that you had vowed not to pick at and then spent an hour popping, squeezing, poking with a pin, rubbing alcohol on and torturing. The kind that you can't cover with make-up and people try to avoid looking at, only they can't because it's so huge! Now you know what I'm talking about and understand my trepidation. She was very sweet and asked me to explain what was going on in my life. I told her I'd just had a baby, was very anxious and was put on anti-anxiety/anti-depressant medication. She asked the magic question, "How do you feel about that?" I told her I felt like a failure and that I couldn't take care of my son. The next magic question, "What makes you think you can't take care of your son?". I didn't have an answer. I was so terrified that I just couldn't take care of him that I hadn't thought about why. The light bulb in my head went on, on dim, but on. She saw it and redirected her questions to my childhood. Like Limony Snicket, my childhood was a series of unfortunate events. The details of which I will not bore you with today. How I reacted to those events and how my parents reacted to those events made me the young woman I was at that moment, struggling to be perfect in everyone's eyes, with no hope of being perfect in my own. And that, my friends, caused enormous amounts of stress. Remember what we said, some stress is good and some stress is bad. This was gnarly, bad, out of control stress. She recommended a counselor for me to see and I followed through with it. The medication reduced the anxiety and empowered me to deal with issues I never could before. I learned why I was the way I was and how to change my thought patterns. I saw a counselor the entire time I was on medication, it worked for me because I couldn't do it alone. I also played Yahtzee by myself when I was super stressed because it was something I thought I could control. In hindsight that was totally irrational, I was playing with dice, but it worked. I was strong enough to know when it was time to move on. She was a "tween" for me. She helped me stand when I was weak and then I found my own two feet. (Wow, that rhymed.) My family and I also went back to church. From that moment on, I've never felt alone. God makes all things possible. He never gives me more than I can bear; he tests my limits mind you, but never more than I can successfully handle with his grace. In a world where nothing is certain except change, I know he loves me. I'd like to share a verse with you that I recite to myself when things get a little stressful: "Be anxious for nothing, but in everything, by prayer and petition, with thanksgiving, present your requests to God. And the peace of God, which transcends all understanding, will guard your hearts and minds in Christ Jesus." (Philippians 4:6–7) Pay particular attention to the first 4 words. God knows how tough it is to be human, trust him.

Anyhoo, today I'm a fantastic, 35-year-old woman that has accepted the "perfection of imperfection". My life isn't stress or trouble free. I live next door to my co-author, his wife and his three sons for pity's sake! Just kidding, I love their family like my own, but the point is, I learned how to deal with issues that cause me stress more effectively. I will admit, certain things still raise my anxiety level. Ants, for example, they totally creep me out. They are small and there's usually a ga-gillion of them and they're fast! Now you all know that this is a "phobia". It's an anxious reaction to a specific trigger. Isn't it fun to learn new things?

Dr. Jekyll's Story

Coffee must always taste the same. When it is made it must have exactly the same amount of sugar, cream, must be stirred the same number of times, and must always be in a particular cup. Not a similar cup. Similar cups are deceptive. If the coffee does not taste the same it is a direct indicator as to how the day will develop. Good coffee—good day. Bad coffee…you get the picture. My argument is that I am not obsessive, but simply very determined and decisive.

All vegetables must be eaten, first, before any meat. If a combination meal is ordered at a drive-thru, the fries must all be eaten first and then the sandwich. Oh yes, the drink must first be tasted before the fries are eaten.

Obsessive-compulsive disorder isn't really obvious until you have studied it and look at your own actions retrospectively. Although my OCD wasn't very severe it is not unusual to find those that have suffered with this to also eventually be blind sided by panic attacks. (I will point out point out, anecdotally, that many physicians have OCD as it can make you extremely detail oriented, thorough, and attentive.)

That Tuesday was a normal day in the world of foot and ankle surgery. It was a hectic day of patients, a surgery, nothing out of the ordinary except one disagreement with another physician. This had happened numerous times before so I never gave it another thought. But something strange happened. About noon, after gulping down a cheeseburger and 44 ounces of a diet beverage (the second of the day) I felt a split second of what can only be described as an "out of body sensation". It was fleeting. Poof and it was gone. I forgot about it. Then a short time later the same thing happened, instantaneous, almost unnoticeable. This happened a few more times before the afternoon of work was finished. It was always the same—an instantaneous, odd sensation—until I arrived home.

I was in the process of training for a marathon. It was my first one and only a month away. If you've ever trained for a marathon you realize that towards the final month running demands a great deal of your evening time. I had running clothes on, something light and sexy—just what I usually run in—and was about to take off out the door when my wife asked if I could take my two oldest sons to their taekwondo practice. That's when it started. I didn't know what it was, but it definitely started. I remember feeling very inconvenienced and then I felt compelled to get up and walk around. My chest felt tight. I remember thinking to myself, "Is this a heart thing?" It got worse. It got to the point where I felt my breathing was labored slightly. I walked from our computer room to the living room. This whole way, which was about twenty feet, it seemed to grow darker. My kids were upstairs getting dressed and my wife was practicing the piano. I'm still not sure how to describe the sensation to someone who has not had a panic attack. The closest I can get is that it is like a cloud, a very dark cloud that seems to surround you and suffocate you. The feeling I first had was, simply put, one of death. My chest was tight. The lights were growing dimmer and my breathing was even more of a struggle. I finally thought to myself, "I have to tell my wife. She may need to call the ambulance." The last thing I managed to do was look at a cross that hangs on our living room wall and saying to myself, "You are going to die." I was scared, but I did make my peace with God and thought, "I hope I can kiss all three of my sons before I die." That's when I half stumbled into our piano room and informed my wife. Naturally we were both thinking physical ailment and most definitely not mental.

It didn't take long for my wife and me to rule out heart disease. Young, active, no family history—it just didn't fit. I still felt so strange. Everytime I looked around I felt as if my eyes weren't lined up. My right eye felt like it was looking at everything about two inches higher than my left eye. It was an odd enough mental sensation that I remember asking her, "Maybe it was a panic attack." This was honestly without knowing what one really was. She immediately looked it up on our computer. (Isn't the internet a grand thing? I bet you can even find a recipe for Lentil soup that requires only blunt objects to make.) It sounded very familiar—"out of the blue", impending doom, strange sensations—the list went on.

I still remember scaring my kids to death when we were leaving for their martial arts class. As we backed out of the garage I sat my cell phone on the dash of the van and asked my oldest son if he knew how to call 911. He assured me that he did. I informed him that I was feeling funny and that if I passed out he was to use my phone to call help. Luckily I fought the sensation off during the short ride and as soon as I arrived home I went next door to describe the details to our good friends Mr. and Mrs. Hyde. (You can recall our description of this encounter earlier in the book.) Even though I felt slightly better because I thought someone else had this experience as well, I still was thinking in the back of my mind, "No, this is different than what you had. This is what people in padded cells feel like". That night I had a scotch and tried to sleep. It was a restless sleep. The sleep where ants are on you, but you awake without red spots—other than in the whites of your eyes. That folks is another bad thing about panic attacks. Sleep deprivation worsens the symptoms and can make you even more anxious.

My career is very important to me and I became convinced that one of two things would happen. I would find out that I really was not having panic attacks, but was really psychotic and would need to be admitted to a hospital. I pictured myself heavily sedated, wearing loose fitting gowns, knitting hats and my three sons visiting me on weekends. I would soil myself and laugh while they were there. They would leave me treats of fresh fruit and herbal teas then go back to school and tell their friends that dad would still be gone on business for another few years. Of course during our visits I would have to wear the oral restraining mask like Hannibal Lector—after all he was a doctor also, so undoubtedly I would also try to eat my children if left unattended. They would wave by to dad and beneath my mask I would also mumble, "Goodbye…next time bring fava beans." (This is disturbing on two levels: one is the obvious level and the other is the fact that fava beans really are not that good.)

The other possibility was that I was not psychotic, but that I truly did suffer from panic disorder, but I would still be deemed unfit for practice. My wife does not work (Outside the home mind you!) so if I were to be stripped of my medical license I would be forced into poverty because I would be unable to maintain a job and the cost of sky-rocketing medication would only make matters worse. It was because of this type of unrealistic fear that I avoided help for 2 months.

My initial attacks continued repetitively for two more days. The most troubling thing was that I had recurring thoughts of, "What if I cannot provide for my family any more?" "What if I were to hurt my family or myself?" I would concentrate. I would read. I would pray. I would drink. Sometimes I would try all at once. Often I would improve, but it seemed within a short time I would be bombarded by more and more thoughts. I can still remember February 4, 2005 vividly. That was the first day a really dark cloud hovered over me for a few hours and I was convinced that on the way home from work I would drive my car off the road. Follow me now. I did not say I wanted to drive myself off the road. I was convinced that I would not be able to control the urge to do so. I did not have the urge, but a fear of having the urge. In desperation I called a local psychiatric hospital. I'm not sure who I spoke with, but even though I wound up not needing their services I would like to say thanks. I did not show up for the appointment later that day, but a woman left a pleasant message on my cell phone asking if I was alright. Thanks anonymous lady. I'm just fine now.

After a few days of this shear misery I did see a family physician, one I knew fairly well, and described the problem. He performed an electrocardiogram to rule out mitral valve prolapse, which can mimic panic attacks, and then placed me on a medication called a beta-blocker. The thought behind use of this type of medication is that it retards the adrenaline response. This may work for someone who is simply "high strung", but in my case it did little except make me extremely tired. I was already tired from the recurrent attacks and the mild depression was causing me to become more lethargic. I succeeded in taking the medicine for only three weeks with worsening of the symptoms.

Each time one of these thoughts erupted into my thoughts I would feel as though I was extremely weak mentally because I could not erase it. (Remember my earlier comment, made in ignorance, about depression and mental weakness.) Regardless of how much I tried, strange and disturbing thoughts would trouble me. To someone that believed most mental illness was largely a choice, I was horrified to feel powerless against controlling these types of thoughts. I struggled with this condition tremendously. I can remember kneeling down in prayer and actually crying so hard there was a large puddle of tears on the hardwood floor of our closet one Tuesday evening. This was only a week after suffering my first attack and I had learned little about the disorder. I was still under the impression that a panic attack was only the intense feeling you experienced for several minutes. I was completely unaware of the other symptoms that accompany these attacks. Experiencing slurred speech and morbid thoughts came as an unexpected shock and convinced me that I had collapsed mentally. The first week I would fall into a fitful sleep every evening around 8:00 p.m. on the sofa. I would wake up multiple times and be convinced that I would not be able continue working, or that I would become a serial killer, or that I would need to be committed into an institution, etc. etc. Within the first week I lost eight pounds and was completely exhausted from lack of sleep.

There would be brief respites of calm that would last for several hours to one or two days at a time. It was during these times that I would glimpse a ray from the sunshine of recovery and I would be encouraged, but quickly this would fade. I began to notice that at times when I was most occupied, such as at work, I wrestled much less with my newly encountered foe. However, anytime that I was not occupied I would quickly feel the fog of depression (and it did actually feel like a fog) creeping in. I would begin to feel overwhelmed and that I would never be happy and enjoy my life again. There were times when I still sweated from trying to concentrate on positive things. At times I would manage to overcome some of the negative images only to have them return with a vengeance. The thoughts would range from beginning to fear that I would not be able to practice medicine to feeling that I had too much in common with various criminals.

My co-author suggested I seek treatment several times, but each time I would see some improvement and convince myself that recovery was around the corner and that professional help was not needed. I called a psychiatric clinic two times, during the first few weeks, because again I really wasn't convinced I had "just" panic attacks. I made an appointment with a psychiatrist and cancelled it when I improved for a weekend.

After two months of avoiding it, I finally kept the appointment with a psychiatrist. In hindsight, the two reasons I had avoided the appointment was that I did not want to jeopardize my career and I felt that I had failed in my level of faith. I felt immediately at ease when the psychiatrist looked at me after he closed the door behind us and said, "Panic attacks huh? Buddy those things are real."

Can I get an amen? They are real. He initially prescribed a gradually decreasing dose of an anxiolytic and a gradually increasing dose of an anti-depressant. The effects of the first medicine were immediate and, again, a wonderful respite. If you have had this constant feeling of "I may lose it" and then you haven't had this feeling, you know what a tremendous relief it can be. I had already learned to ignore the majority of my physiological reactions. The most common of these was an increased heart rate, an inability to concentrate, and a medicine head type feeling. The anti-depressant took a few weeks to really take effect, but as I decreased the dose of the relaxing medicine it became effective at the perfect time.

Now I'm writing a book about it. Why am I writing a book? Is it the windfall of fame and fortune that will undoubtedly accompany its publication? Partially. Mostly, however, I remember how I felt for several weeks and I would wish that feeling on no one. In all of my reading I only found somber accounts of personal stories. I am not a somber person by nature. Humor, even juvenile humor, can be very healing. It has also been a source of therapy for me as well. After reading on this and related topics extensively. It is clear, now, that the whole panic disorder had been building for a while.

At this point I have set this book aside for a few months and feel perfectly normal. In fact, the whole panic attack thing seems like a bad dream at this point. I do not experience any of the physiological symptoms such as a racing heart beat. Every now and then I'll have a day when I feel a little bummed and I wonder if I'm slipping backwards, but I'm not. Today I write not as someone who is cured, but as someone who can finally see mostly blue sky and only an occasional glimpse of the anxiety goblin. Soon I anticipate incorporating the flatulence enhancing techniques and expect complete recovery.

The Innocent and Confused Bystander

The bystander can be anyone. A spouse, a girlfriend, a boyfriend, a family member or even the neighbor next door we discussed earlier. When your spouse comes to you and claims they think they're going crazy, there are two ways to react to this. (Well probably more than two but who has time to count ways of reacting when you're reacting?) The first is to talk in a very controlled, monotone voice while backing up slowly, checking out all possible exits and counting the kitchen knives silently in your head, all the while telling them "you're not crazy…it's everyone else…they're crazy." At this point it's your call whether you make a mad dash to the nearest door or pick up the phone and call the local psych ward. The upside of this reaction is chances are fairly good that you'll live to see another day. That is of course if you don't get hit by a car while running for your life or get wrapped up in the telephone cord and accidentally hang yourself. These things, while possible, are not probable.

The second reaction is to be supportive and nurturing. It's probably the most overlooked option of the two, but it does have it's benefits as well. One benefit is that chances are good you will live to see another day. Yes, it was a benefit for the first reaction but let's be honest. You can never overuse the benefit of living another day. As reactions go, I chose the latter…mostly! I chose this not because I understood what she was going through or I thought I could *fix* her. I chose this because running for cover or having to fill out paperwork to have her committed seemed liked a lot of work and I really wasn't up for it. Who knew my laziness was supportiveness in disguise.

I say "mostly" because at times when I was saying out loud "don't worry honey, you're gonna be alright." inside I was saying "Isn't it about time you got over this? How long are you gonna milk this anyway?" "What about ME?" Yes the guilt of being insincere was uncomfortable at times but you get over it quickly when you have to leave public places and social gatherings because they're having another "episode." (Do you know how many unfinished beers I've had to leave behind! It wasn't a pretty picture)

If you've never been exposed to someone experiencing anxiety there are certain "clues" that will tip you off that your spouse is going through it. I remember some of my wife's moods. They were…what's the word…ah yes…interesting. There were times when she would come home from work and play board games for hours on end. ALL BY HERSELF. (clue) Far be it for me to criticize someone who's working on perfecting a skill but it becomes a little unsettling to hear someone whisper "yahtzee" to themselves while slowly looking over their shoulder making sure no one was there to verify it. Trying to blow it off, I'd ask if I could play. She would tell me that she'd love for me to play but there were already too many players (clue)

There were also times when she said she couldn't get comfortable because her clothes felt too tight. I know a lot of women say things like this but not many say it when they are only wearing flip flops. (clue) Then there times when commercials would make her cry for what seemed liked forever. Many people, present company included, cry at commercials. The difference is that most of us can hold it together when the little lizard comes on and tells us to call for cheaper insurance. I gotta say…not much of a tear jerker!! (clue) If your spouse is displaying any of these tell-tale signs you could be living with someone who's going through anxiety.

Although my wife felt like she was going crazy, I knew otherwise. The tough part about being the spouse of someone experiencing anxiety and having panic attacks, is to get them to understand they're not going crazy. What's tougher is, when reality hits and you realize you aren't able to *fix* them! You go into this mode of trying to rationalize everything or of having all the answers. You start treating them like a child that is unable to take care of themselves.

This happens more often to us guys because let's face it…that's how we are! Our egos need for us to be the hero. You need to be careful that you don't get caught up in this for too long. By being the saver all of the time you could be creating bigger problems in the long run. Like having your spouse lose the ability to take care of themselves. Helpless damsels are a thing of the past. You need to move on. Treating your spouse like a problem to be solved instead of someone who needs your understanding isn't going to do either or you any good.

That's not to say that women deal with their husbands any better. They probably do, but I'm not saying it! The women (or woman) I know who's husband experienced panic attacks handled it a little differently then I did. She went out and spent a lot of money. I mean A LOT of money. I believe this was in an effort to take her husband's mind off of "his problems" so he could focus on something else…her. I'll admit, the concept of spending a lot of money does sound very appealing. If I was in a position to do it, that may have been the route I took. I don't believe it had the medicinal effect that she was looking for so it's probably a good thing I didn't have that option. I don't want to sound like I'm being overly critical of my friend. She does and will always love her husband very much and handled this the best way she knew how. Her approach to dealing was just different then mine.

The whole point of this chapter is to make you aware that when your spouse starts displaying panic attacks, don't over react. They're not doing it to be a pain in your butt even if that is how it comes across. They're as confused as you are. You're not expected to fix them, you just have to be there for them. Although I couldn't fix my wife I could help her get through it. I did this by listening to her. I could not understand what she was feeling, but I could hear what she was feeling. To let her know that whatever she told me was O.K., even if I didn't get it. To have her educate me, while educating herself, about how she felt, when she felt it and what made her feel that way. In some cases, this was enough to lessen the attacks.

Lessen maybe, but not stop completely. Professionals can help for the long haul. Professional counselors, psychologist, psychiatrist, philanthropist. Alright, you got me. A philanthropist can't help. Well maybe if your spouses panic attacks were brought on by ungenerous people then it would be helpful to have a philanthropist or two on hand just in case.

Sit down with them and have them create a list of what they're fearing the most and then talking about the chances of those things happening. Fears that before they'd never focus on are now a big part of their thought process. How do you relate to that? You don't, you just need to be there for them…completely. Sometimes all you can do is give them a big hug. You may be tempted to hug around the neck region. Although this may be mentally satisfying, the physical reality won't be the same . It is highly discouraged and can be very impractical.

Again, these aren't cures, but brief moments in which the pain can be eased. This is where it may have dawned on you that it's not gonna be easy. You got it. It's not easy for them or you. If treated though, it can be corrected. I'm happy to say that my wife has not had a panic attack or anxiety for many years now. She gets a little freakish every now and then. That's when I know she's back to her ol' self.

Conclusion

It has been stated, "That which does not kill us makes us stronger." It has also been said, "A monkey on your back makes your legs bigger." The authors agree that essentially these quotes (One authentic—the other constructed under the influence of heavy caffeine usage.) mean the same thing. Even though one of our journeys is not quite complete, we have both become stronger and most likely better people for what we have been through. Dealing with panic attacks has encouraged us to become more empathetic, more caring, and more resilient. If you seek proof of this ask yourself, "Would my authors have troubled themselves to have produced this fine academic specimen I am reading if they had never had a panic attack?"

As you research this disorder it is unlikely that you will find a better book. Granted you may find better "content", more appropriate uses of "metaphors", "easier" and "more effective" methods of relaxation, superior "education", a "greater understanding" of the problem, and "high quality writing", but aside from those few things, our book is unbeatable. So place it on the coffee table. Lay it near your bed. Put a copy near household toilets and one in the glove box of your automobile. Above all give a copy to a fellow sufferer or someone you want to educate without terrifying.

In retrospect this book has not turned out to be simply humorous. Our original intent was to make you soil yourself with laughter, but the more we wrote, the more we realized that there would have to be some serious parts because it's based on our personal experiences. A pre publication review that we solicited cautioned us about trying to be experts and also on our religious content. The review was actually very helpful, but we decided that we really just disagreed. We are experts because we have lived through it and religion played a dominant role in our recovery. To downplay religion because it may be too serious compared to other parts of the book would be dishonest.

Your authors leave you with two points to remember. First, once you have recovered—and we believe you will recover—make a concerted effort to help someone else. It may be another "panic attacker" or it may be someone who just needs a word of encouragement at the right time. You will be amazed at how focusing on others draw our attention away from ourselves and can actually improve our own situation. Last, remember that Jekyll and Hyde coined the terms "*illegitimate stress*" and "*panic attackers*".

978-0-595-36569-2
0-595-36569-8